Grandpa's
FORTUNE
Fables

If you think of
money like seeds,
you will be able to

ACHIEVE GREAT WEALTH

YOU JUST HAVE TO FOLLOW
THREE RULES:

1. KEEP ONE OUT OF EVERY TEN SEEDS YOU RECEIVE
2. PLANT THE SEEDS YOU KEEP
3. LET YOUR TREES **GROW**

GRANDPA JACK

This first edition published in 2021

This book is one of the resources, to help parents teach their kids about money, provided by the financial education company:
Blue Tree Savings Ltd
83 Ducie Street
Manchester
M1 2JQ

Printed and bound in United Kingdom

ISBN 978-1-7399726-0-8
eISBN 978-1-7399726-2-2

Cover design: Andrew Salisbury and Cleriston Ribeiro
Book design and chapter titles: Andrew Salisbury
Illustrations: Cleriston Ribeiro

This book is dedicated to:

My kids, Imogen and Florence, who inspired me to write these stories.

My parents for showing me the benefits of saving money.

My wife, Astrid, for supporting and encouraging me as I created this book, my course, and my website (bluetreesavings.com).

Contents

CAN YOU SOLVE GRANDPA'S MYSTERY CODE?

As you read this book, and discover the secrets of money, you'll find a question at the end of each chapter for you to answer.

Select the correct answer and put the letter (which is next to the answer) in the corresponding place below to solve the code.

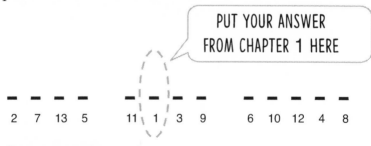

PUT YOUR ANSWER FROM CHAPTER 1 HERE

2 7 13 5   11 1 3 9   6 10 12 4 8

Chapter numbers

See if you have cracked the code and receive your prize by going to: **www.fortune-club.co.uk**

Part 1

BECOMING

Wealthy

THE BULLY!
EVERYONE CAN BECOME WEALTHY

"WHAT ARE YOU DOING TO MY FLOWERS!" shouted Gail as she ran over to the patch where a boy was kicking the tops off the flowers.

"What does it look like?! Get out of here **DORK**!" yelled the boy, who was wearing an old leather jacket.

As he turned to look at her, she immediately recognised him. It was Boris Duckworth.

Despite only being thirteen years old, Boris was notorious for being the village bully. At school he'd pick on someone simply because he thought it was a funny thing to do. If you didn't think it was funny, then you'd be the next one he'd pick on!

Luckily for Gail, whilst she was the same age as Boris, she went to the other school in their village.

Just before she was about to react to Boris calling her a **DORK**!, Gail remembered something her Grandpa had once told her: "Bullies bully people as they have been bullied themselves. They don't see happiness in their lives and can't stand to see other people happy."

It was well known that Boris' parents were really mean to him. One time Boris got a small piece of chewing gum stuck in his hair. The next thing he knew, his mum dragged him to the barber, crying, and had him shave off all of Boris' hair.

Gail decided that rather than just shouting back at Boris, she'd try a different approach. "ACTUALLY . . . please carry on kicking my flowers. Saves me a job! I need to take the petals off those flowers to make money anyway!"

Boris didn't know what to do or say. He wanted to keep kicking the flowers, but he didn't want to do as he was told.

"YOU'RE LYING!" Boris blurted. "You can't make money from these flowers I've just killed."

"Then please carry on. As I said, you're actually helping me," said Gail with a smirk.

It was then Boris realised who she was.

"I know you. You're the girl with all the money and the super-rich grandparents!" hollered Boris.

It wasn't easy to tell that Gail had a lot of money from looking at her. She was a 'geek', 'nerd', 'dork' or whatever other word you can think of for someone who cares more about learning new things than being 'cool'. Unlike many of her geeky friends, she was confident and proud to be a nerd (which, in a strange way, actually made her cool). Most days she'd wear a t-shirt with some dorky quote on it, like **"FROM A SINGLE SEED, A FOREST CAN GROW!"**.

"You're so lucky to have been GIVEN all that money so you can do whatever you want," said Boris as he kicked another bunch of flowers.

"I haven't been given any money for many years. I have earned and grown my money myself," replied Gail.

"YOU CAN'T GROW MONEY! Haven't your parents told you that money doesn't grow on trees?" returned Boris.

"My grandpa told me that whilst money doesn't grow on trees, it can grow like trees," Gail fired back.

Gail wanted to tell Boris what her grandpa had told her about money, but she was still angry at him for kicking her flowers and being so rude —not to mention her dislike for bullies in general. At the same time, she wanted to help him because of how his parents treated him.

Gail composed herself and said, "I'll make you a deal. If you help me pick up all the petals from the flowers you've kicked, and put them in this bag, I'll share with you what my grandpa taught me about the secrets of money. You never know, these secrets might help you grow up to be wealthy!"

Picking up petals didn't appeal to Boris at all. However, the thought of learning the secrets of money got him really excited. He looked around to make sure there weren't any other kids around. "OK – only because I want to be **RICH**. This better not be a trick!" said Boris.

Gail smiled to herself when she saw the boy everyone was afraid of, picking up the petals, which she was then going to use to make some money with.

As they worked together, Gail explained that during her summer holidays, she'd stay at her grandparents' house. Whilst there, her grandpa enjoyed nothing more than sharing the amazing tales of how he discovered the secrets of money on his adventure to the island of Pucha-Pucha. These secrets led her grandpa to becoming one of the wealthiest people in the country.

In fact, Gail's school, **THE FITZGERALD MIDDLE SCHOOL**, was actually named after her grandparents as they would use their money to make generous donations to local charities.

"You are so lucky. I've never been taught about money," said Boris. He sighed as he stuffed handfuls of petals into the bag. "My parents have never seemed to have any money, despite both working. The only time I hear them talking about money is when they are arguing. Whenever I ask if I can have some money they bark, **'Why would we give you any of our money?'**".

Gail told Boris, "Like most people, your parents were probably never taught about money. That might be why they argue about money. I'm happy to tell you everything my grandpa taught me about money. You see, when my grandpa was growing up, his family never had any money."

"You're joking! Your grandpa came from a family that didn't have a lot of money? There's no way I can become as **RICH** as your grandpa," replied Boris.

"Let's go to the Burger Shack to grab a drink. I can then tell you how my grandpa discovered the secrets of money. You'll see that if you follow my grandpa's **Three Rules of Wealth** then you can become WEALTHY just like him."

Discuss with your Parents, Class and Friends
(real or imaginary)

Why do you think Gail was so kind to Boris even though he was a bully?

GRANDPA'S
MYSTERY CODE (1)

Answer the question below and put the letter in the corresponding place on page 1 to solve the code.

"For Boris to become wealthy, he needs to the learn the ___"?

O: Three Rules of Wealth

E: Seven Days of the Week

A: Five Best Ways to Spend Money

GRANDPA'S GOLD

GETTING RICH QUICK

When Boris and Gail got to the Burger Shack, Gail ordered her favourite, a strawberry milkshake with whipped cream on top.

"Boris, what would you like? My treat," said Gail.

"*YOU'RE GOING TO BUY ME A DRINK?*

Why? I just killed your flowers," said Boris. No one had ever offered to buy Boris a drink before.

"Remember, I'm going to make money from those petals so think of this as a thank you for helping me collect them," replied Gail.

Boris didn't question it anymore and ordered a chocolate milkshake.

Once they'd got their drinks, Gail told Boris about how her grandpa had learned the secrets of money and become extremely wealthy on his adventure to the island of Pucha-Pucha.

GRANDPA'S GOLD STORY

When Grandpa Jack was young, his family had very little money and he had to share a small bedroom with his three brothers. Every day was a struggle and he never really got on with his brothers; they all picked on him as he was the youngest.

Grandpa left school at sixteen to go work in a newspaper printing factory with his father and brothers. He would pick up the freshly printed newspapers and put them on the lorries for delivery. Every day was exactly the same. It was soooo boring. Whilst he was only sixteen, he felt his dreams of exploring the world were never going to happen.

Then, shortly after his seventeenth birthday, he picked up a newspaper and saw the headline:

Grandpa thought this was his opportunity to change his future and see the world.

"I'm going to go to Pucha-Pucha to find gold. **I'M GOING TO BE RICH!!!**" shouted Grandpa, causing three people in the coffee room to spill their drinks.

He left a note for his parents telling them that he'd gone to Pucha-Pucha and would come back a rich man!

The big problem was that he didn't have enough money to get to the island. Luckily, he remembered his Uncle Louis was a fisherman.

Uncle Louis offered to take him there on his boat. The only downside was that he'd have to listen to his uncle's awful jokes for three days non-stop.

Grandpa was willing to do whatever it took to get to the island. He threw his bag on the boat and they set sail.

As soon as they left the dock his uncle started with the jokes.

"I ONLY KNOW TWENTY-FIVE LETTERS IN THE ALPHABET ... I DON'T KNOW 'Y'"

"WHAT DO YOU CALL A COW DURING AN EARTHQUAKE? ... A MILKSHAKE!"

"WHAT KIND OF NOISE DOES A WITCH'S VEHICLE MAKE? ... BRRROOOOMM, BRRROOOMM!"

The jokes got worse as the trip went on.

In the moments where he wasn't having to pretend to laugh at his uncle's jokes, Grandpa kept thinking of all the places he would explore once he found gold on the island.

They finally arrived on Pucha-Pucha at the same time as a big ship sailed into the dock. The big ship was carrying what seemed like hundreds of travellers. They'd all come with the hope of finding gold. As they got off the ship, they were greeted by a loud and handsome man named Sam.

"Welcome All!"

Sam shouted with his booming voice, "Who here wants to become rich beyond their wildest dreams?"

Everyone raised their hands and shouted,

"ME!" "ME!" "ME!"

"You see that big house on the hill over there?" said Sam, pointing to an amazing house on a lush, green hillside. "A house like that could be all yours tomorrow when you find your gold," continued Sam. "Now go buy a shovel from my store and find your gold!"

All the travellers were so keen to get started that they hurried to the store and paid what little money they had to buy their shovels.

After getting his shovel, Grandpa ran into the hills where there weren't any other travellers. He wanted to make sure that if he found some gold, he'd be able to keep it for himself.

He started **digging, digging, digging** but found no gold. Tomorrow would surely be better.

Sadly, Grandpa didn't find any gold the next day or the day after that or the day after that.

Grandpa was quickly running out of food. **"I'M SO HUNGRY,"** he'd say to himself. He then looked up and saw the big house on the hill and said, "I will find gold and have a house like that one day!" He kept digging but still couldn't find any gold.

Grandpa started wandering around in search of food, feeling desperately tired and lonely. He even started to miss his uncle's terrible jokes.

Just as he was about to sit down to get some rest, he saw some light coming from a small farmhouse in the distance. He used the little energy he had left to run over to the house.

Knock! Knock!

An old but spritely man opened the door. "Hello there! Can I help you?" He then saw how tired and hungry Grandpa looked and didn't wait for a reply before saying, "Come in! Come in! Let me get you some food."

Grandpa smiled and went into the house. The man's house was full of bowls of fruit and vegetables, and he was cooking a stew which smelt amazing.

"You must have been one of the lucky ones to have found gold," exclaimed Grandpa.

"Unfortunately not. There has only ever been one man, **RICHIE RACCOON**, who has ever found gold on this island."

Grandpa was shocked. "What do you mean? We were told that there was plenty of gold and that the big house is owned by someone who found gold on this island."

"That's what they want you to think! That house belongs to Shovel Sam," said the man. "Sam didn't find any gold. When he found out

that **RICHIE RACCOON** had found gold, Sam started telling all the newspapers from around the world that there was gold on Pucha-Pucha. Thousands of people have come here looking for gold so they could get rich quick, and each of them has bought a shovel from Sam. Shovel Sam's now the richest person on the island."

Grandpa felt sorry for himself. His desire to get rich quick had led him to be easily tricked by Sam, like so many others.

WHAT'S A SCAM?

Gail told Boris that there's a lot of people who want to '**get rich quick**' and are likely to fall for tricks, just like when Grandpa got tricked, or '𝕊ℂ𝔸𝕄𝕄𝔼𝔻,' by Sam.

"As my grandpa now always reminds me, 'If someone tells you that you can make money quickly, they are probably scamming you and getting rich themselves!" said Gail.

Like many people who have been tricked, Gail's grandpa didn't want to believe that it was a scam and was determined to find gold. He said to himself "If that man, **RICHIE RACCOON**, can find gold on this island then so can I. I'm not going to give up. I will find gold and become rich."

Grandpa never found gold, but through his sheer determination to uncover it, he discovered the secrets of money which made him extremely wealthy.

Discuss with your Parents, Class, Friends and ... a goldfish

Why do you think it was so easy for Shovel Sam to trick so many people?

GRANDPA'S
MYSTERY CODE (2)

Answer the question below and put the letter in the corresponding place on page 1 to solve the code.

Which word below means "To be tricked out of money"?

T: Shovelled

S: Scammed

R: Clowned

CHAPTER 3

Richie Raccoon
RICH VS WEALTHY

Boris was now eager to learn what Gail's grandpa did to earn so much money.

"Let me guess, your grandpa started selling shovels like Sam and that's how he became super-rich!" said Boris, half joking and half worried he was right.

"No, no! Grandpa would never do that. He's an honest man, he likes to help people, not trick them. Let me explain what happened after Grandpa had been scammed."

Richie Raccoon vs. Wealthy Wallaby

It had been two months since Grandpa had travelled to Pucha-Pucha looking for gold. He had dug everywhere on the island, but hadn't had any luck.

As he was travelling around digging for gold, all he had to eat was the fruit growing on the trees. Some days he spent more time looking for food than he spent DIGGING for gold. He found a fruit tree and then made the best decision ever, which ultimately ended up changing his life in so many ways.

Instead of eating all of the fruits, he took some of them, cut them open and took out the seeds. He then planted the seeds in the ground. He wanted to have a place on the island where he knew he would be able to find fruit. The best way to ensure that was to start growing his own.

For every ten fruits he was lucky enough to find, he kept one, harvesting the seeds from it and planting them near his other fruit trees.

After he had planted the seeds, he continued his search for gold. It was hard. He was so hungry that he just wanted to eat all the fruit, but he didn't. **HE KEPT SAVING ONE OUT OF EVERY TEN HE FOUND.**

His days of digging and only eating a few fruits started to get Grandpa down. What made those early days even harder was when he bumped into **RICHIE RACCOON**. That wasn't his real name, but people called him that because he would dig like a raccoon and he was the only one on the island to find gold, so he was rich.

Richie wasn't a nice man. He'd always be well dressed in new clothes and dark sunglasses (which he'd keep losing). Richie loved to brag about the nice meals that he had eaten to everyone he met.

"Hey **Wimpy Wallaby** (which is the name Richie gave to Grandpa as he was so slim and the way he would bounce around the island hopelessly looking for gold), found any gold yet? I bet you haven't. **HA HA HA HA HA HA HA HA HA HA HA HA HA HA HA HA HA HA HA HA HA HA HA,**" teased Richie as he passed by.

Grandpa didn't react. After growing up fighting with his brothers, he knew fighting only ended up with him getting hurt and in trouble.

Deep down Grandpa felt he needed to find gold to be as happy as Richie Raccoon.

Grandpa would DIG DIG DIG, but still wouldn't find any gold.

Luckily, as the weeks passed, his fruit trees were now producing lots of fruit. He decided to trade some of his fruit for some chickens and after many months he even got a cow. As he could not eat all the eggs from the chickens and the milk from the cow, he would sell some to people in the village. The good thing was that his trees, chickens and cow kept providing him with things to sell each day. He was now making a lot of money, although, he made sure he kept planting one out of every ten seeds he got.

Grandpa was now free to do what he wanted with his time. He even had enough money to buy some new clothes, like **RICHIE RACCOON** wore.

It was then that he noticed that he hadn't seen Richie for some time. Grandpa decided to go and find him to make sure he was OK. He assumed he was fine as he knew Richie had enough gold to be able to buy a whole forest like his if he'd wanted.

When Grandpa did finally find Richie, it turned out he wasn't doing so well.

"Hey Richie, are you alright? You look really tired."

"No. I'm not doing alright at all," snapped Richie. "I've not managed to find any gold for a month now. As I'd spent all the gold I found before, I haven't been able to eat a proper meal in ages. I'M SO HUNGRY."

Despite Grandpa not liking Richie, he felt sorry for him. He invited him back to his home and gave him some food.

Richie was so thankful to Grandpa. He said, "I can't believe you are being so kind to me given that I've always teased you. I'm so sorry for calling you **Wimpy Wallaby**. Look at this forest you have grown, it must be worth a fortune. You are certainly looking after your money better than I ever did. I wish I had a 'FORTUNE FOREST' like yours! I shall now call you *Wealthy Wallaby*!!"

Richie decided that he would start to grow his own 'Fortune Forest'.

WHAT'S THE DIFFERENCE BETWEEN "RICH" AND "WEALTHY"?

Grandpa would often tell Gail about Richie, especially as there were so many people like **RICHIE RACCOON** in the world. They have nice houses, fast cars, and fancy clothes. They always appear to have enough money to buy whatever they want. The truth, in fact, is as they spend all their money, they aren't saving any of it — like Richie never saved any of his gold.

If you have money and spend it all, then you might be RICH, like **RICHIE RACCOON**. If you save and grow your money, then you will become **WEALTHY**, like Wealthy Wallaby (Grandpa).

"I never knew about saving money. I only ever see my parents spending money, like Richie did," said Boris.

"Ever since my grandpa told me that story, I have been saving one dollar out of every ten dollars I receive—like my grandpa did with his fruit," replied Gail.

"So, your grandpa is super wealthy because he sold fruits, eggs and milk when he was on the island?" asked Boris with a puzzled expression on his face.

"Sort of. After eight years on **Pucha-Pucha**, Grandpa ended up selling his Fortune Forest and sailed back home to his family. When he got back home, he used the money he had left over and applied the **Three Rules of Wealth** that he learned from growing his

Fortune Forest, to become super wealthy," said Gail.

"Come on, you've got to tell me these rules. I really want to know!" said Boris.

"Before I tell you the rules, you need to **LEARN HOW TO EARN MONEY.** My grandpa told me an awesome story that has helped me start earning a lot more money than most kids. Let's meet here tomorrow so I can tell you his story," Gail said enthusiastically.

Discuss with your Parents, Class, Friends and ...
favourite teacher

Why do you think it is important to save some of your money?

GRANDPA'S
MYSTERY CODE (3)

Answer the question below and put the letter in the corresponding place on page 1 to solve the code.

Which word below means "Someone who has money saved and is growing their money over time"?

U: Wealthy

O: Rich

W: Poor

Part 2

EARNING
Money

WORKING SMART

As Gail walked up to the **burger shack** to meet Boris, she saw a little boy running towards her crying. She stopped the boy to ask what had happened.

"The big **BULLY** in there took my pocket money!" cried the boy.

Gail knew exactly who the big bully was. It was Boris! Just as she had started to feel sorry for him, he went and did something like this.

"GIVE THIS BOY HIS MONEY BACK!" demanded Gail as she confronted Boris.

Everyone was shocked to see the small, dorky girl standing up to Boris.

Boris didn't know what to do. He needed to keep up his tough guy appearance in front of his goon friends.

"I was only playing with him. Of course, I was going to give him his money back!" replied Boris, pretending to be joking.

Gail immediately left the Burger Shack and started walking back home.

Boris ran after her. "I'm really sorry, I shouldn't have done that. My friends like it when I'm mean to other kids. They think I'm funny," he admitted.

"You need to get new friends if they only like you when you are a bully," said Gail, still angry with Boris.

"Please, I really want to hear more of your grandpa's stories. If I don't learn then I'll never be able to change."

That last comment took Gail by surprise. Boris was admitting that he needed to change and that took a lot of courage.

"I'm only going to keep telling you my grandpa's stories if you promise that you won't bully any kids again. **Do we have a deal?**" said Gail.

"I'll prove how serious I am about this. Here, you can have my leather jacket. I only wear it to make me look tough like some of the hard kids on TV."

Gail couldn't believe it. "**Wow**. I won't take your jacket, but the fact that you are willing to give it to me shows me how serious you are. I'll keep telling you my grandpa's stories but this is your last chance."

"Thank you. I'm glad you didn't actually take my jacket as my mum would have shouted at me," Boris said with a smile.

They walked to the nearby park, away from Boris' 'friends', and sat together on a bench. There, Gail continued to tell Boris about her grandpa's journey to become the country's WEALTHIEST PERSON.

"Remember that my grandpa started off selling fresh fruits, eggs and milk from the forest he had grown? Well, he did that after hearing a story about two farmers who lived on Pucha-Pucha. He learned that it's not only about working hard; you have to work smart too!"

HAPPY FARMER, SAD FARMER STORY

There was once a farmer called Sid. People on Pucha-Pucha called him **Sad Sid** as he was always very grumpy. He would work on his farm all day picking strawberries, no matter how bad the weather. If someone was willing to listen to him, he'd gladly complain about his life to them all day, every day. Particularly, he'd complain about his neighbour **Happy Hannah.**

Hannah was also a farmer on the island. She picked strawberries like Sid did, but didn't work as many hours. She also had a nice house— much nicer than Sid's. She'd pay people to pick most of her **STRAWBERRIES**. She also went on nice fishing trips with her happy family. Everyone except Sid liked Hannah.

Sid didn't think it was fair that Hannah had everything, and he had so little, especially as he worked so hard. To Sid, Hannah was **SOOO LUCKY!!**

Then one day, a massive storm hit the island. Both Hannah's and Sid's strawberry fields and homes were destroyed.

Once the storm was over, Hannah had to go back to growing and picking strawberries herself. This made Sid very happy, and he thought to himself, "Finally, Hannah isn't getting all the luck. Now she's in the same position as me!"

Both Sid and Hannah started working and earned money based on the number of strawberries they grew, picked, and could sell at the market.

Three months after the storm had ended, their strawberries had regrown and were ready for picking. As Sid was faster at picking strawberries, he managed to sell more strawberries and earn more money than Hannah. **THIS MADE SID A BIT HAPPIER.**

That night, Sid had a nice meal whilst Hannah only had a basic meal.

The next day Sid started picking more strawberries from his farm. Hannah got up early to pick strawberries, but she now had a small tool in her hand. It was a metal glove with a small blade on the thumb. She had spent most of the previous evening designing and making the tool; she had used the earnings she had saved by only having a basic meal to buy the metal parts she needed. The tool allowed her to pick a lot more strawberries than before, but in the same amount of time.

At the end of the next day, Hannah had managed to pick and sell more strawberries than Sid due to the tool she had made. This made Sid **grumpy** again!

Sid had another nice meal. He could see that Hannah's meal wasn't as nice as his. Sid couldn't work out why! She had earned more money, so why was she still not having a nice meal?!

The next day Sid got up to start working on his farm as usual. This time, Hannah arrived with two other people. They were working with her and both had the tool Hannah had designed. Sid didn't know how she could afford it. She would have to share her earnings between the three of them. However, Hannah and her helpers had managed to pick over five times as many strawberries as Sid had.

Rather than selling all of her **STRAWBERRIES**, Hannah kept some strawberries for herself.

Sid couldn't understand why she would want to keep the strawberries.

When the next day came, Sid arrived at the strawberry fields as usual, although even more grumpy than before. He saw Hannah's helpers, plus two new ones, but there was no sign of Hannah herself.

When it was lunchtime, he noticed a lot of people walking to the local village. He asked them why they were going there. They said, **"Haven't you heard!** A new store has opened today selling super fresh and delicious strawberry drinks and snacks!"

Sid went to the store and couldn't believe his eyes. Hannah was there selling the drinks and snacks she had made with the strawberries she had left over.

Then Sid noticed that some of the helpers weren't picking strawberries, but were planting new crops. These grew into other types of fruit.

Before long, Hannah had stores all over the island, selling a range of fruit drinks and snacks. Also, Hannah learned an important lesson from what happened due to the **STORM** and made things that didn't rely on growing strawberries all year round. She started making jams and nice fruit bowls. If there was another storm, she'd still have things to sell and make money from.

Hannah left the running of the shops to other people which meant she had more time to spend with her (once again) happy family.

Soon enough they were back to the same place they'd started: **Sad Sid** and **Happy Hannah**. Sid realised that Hannah wasn't lucky. She worked hard and worked smart. She focused on how to put the money she earned to good use so she could earn more money.

Soon Sad Sid copied Hannah's ideas. He asked Hannah for her tool design (which she was happy to share) and then got help. He didn't like the basic meals he knew he had to eat, but it wasn't long before he too was eating slightly more exciting meals and having all the freedom that Hannah had.

GAIL EXPLAINS THAT MONEY CAN HELP MAKE MORE MONEY

Gail told Boris that when Grandpa was on Pucha-Pucha, he wanted to be more like **Happy Hannah**. Instead of spending all his money buying clothes and nice meals, he used some of the money to buy some chickens and then a cow so he could earn even more money.

"Apparently, he even started to make wooden highchairs from his trees, but that's a story he wants to tell me more about one day!" said Gail.

"My parents spend all their money," snapped Boris. "I have no idea about how to make money. That probably doesn't surprise you as I'm not exactly the **smartest kid** around."

"Don't put yourself down. You've just never been taught. I had no idea how to earn money until my grandpa helped me. Since then, I've been using those flowers that you were rudely kicking when we first met to make money."

"Sorry about that," Boris said as he gave an apologetic smile. "I still have no clue how you are going to make money from those flowers."

"Let me call home to let them know I'll be back late. I'LL TELL YOU HOW I MAKE MONEY FROM THOSE FLOWERS," replied Gail.

Discuss with your Parents, Class, Friends and ...
the person in the mirror

Why do you think Happy Hannah decided to spend her evening creating a new tool rather than just relaxing?

GRANDPA'S
MYSTERY CODE (4)

Answer the question below and put the letter in the corresponding place on page 1 to solve the code.

Which of the below means "Thinking of ideas to make things better or easier"?

E: Working Smart

I: Working Hard

O: Working Slowly

KID ENTREPRENEUR

"Before I tell you about how I made money from those flowers you were kicking, let me tell you about the **POCKET MONEY** my parents gave me when I was really young. This allowed me to learn some really important money lessons," said Gail.

GAIL'S POCKET MONEY

Many people believe that my grandparents gave a lot of money to my parents and they gave money to me. That's not exactly the case.

Saying that, when I was four years old, they started to give me weekly pocket money.

Even though the amount was small, my parents encouraged me to start saving a little bit each week, just like Grandpa saved one out of every ten fruits he received on **Pucha-Pucha**. Saving a bit of money is now a habit which will make me wealthy in the future. Without that pocket money, it would have been hard to form the habit of saving.

As I got older, I wanted to find ways to earn more. That's when I started going to my grandpa's house to learn how to earn money.

One day I went to my grandpa's house, he was busy in his garden. I asked him how I could earn more money. I was thinking he'd give me some jobs around the garden and give me a bit of money once I'd finished.

"If I give you a job, you'll be like **Sad Sid** and be working hard for money. Why don't you think of ways to make money by being like **Happy Hannah?** Maybe you could create something to sell," said Grandpa. He was referring back to the 'Happy Farmer, Sad Farmer' story he had recently told me.

"But I don't have anything to sell," I replied.

"There are always opportunities to create something new. Look around you. I'm sure if you use your **AMAZING IMAGINATION**, you can find something to make which your friends would love," said Grandpa as he went back to clearing up his flower beds.

I didn't have any idea what I could create. All I could see were flower petals lying on the ground. I started to get frustrated that my grandpa made it seem so simple. I collected the petals and wrote out, "I HAVE NO IDEA" using them.

Grandpa came over and said, "Young Lady, I think you've just come up with something!"

I was super confused. "What have I come up with?"

"Have you ever seen a sign made from flower petals? I haven't. It looks different and very colourful. I'd love to have a sign or picture like that in a frame," stated Grandpa.

I looked at the "**I HAVE NO IDEA**" petal sign and saw that he was right. It was colourful and unique.

We then started to collect as many of the fallen petals as possible. I started to make different signs and pictures. My grandpa then gave me an old picture frame so I could put one of my favourite pictures in the frame. The glass kept the petals in place. **It looked so cool.**

The next day I took my picture to school to show my friends. They loved it and wanted me to make them one.

I rushed back to my grandpa's house to tell him the good news. He said I could take as many of the fallen flower petals as I needed.

"I don't have many frames you can use. You'll have to go to the shops to buy some," Grandpa said.

I had **$10** left from my **POCKET MONEY** I'd saved over the last few weeks. Usually, I would use this to go to the cinema, but I figured I could always go to the cinema once I had sold some of my pictures.

I bought five picture frames for **$2** each and made five petal pictures. I managed to sell them all to my friends. They each paid me **$7** which covered the cost of the frames **($10)** and a trip to the cinema **($10)**, and I still had some left over **($15)**.

"What are you going to do with that extra money you made?" Grandpa asked.

"I'M GOING TO BUY MORE FRAMES!" I said excitedly.

I continued to make the pictures. My parents would take us to the car boot sale to sell them there.

Grandpa said he was running out of flower petals in his garden. I then decided to go around the village and ask if people would like help getting rid of the fallen petals from their flowers. They were willing to pay me for doing this so I was earning even more money, plus I got to keep the fallen petals to make more pictures and earn even more money.

I used some of the money to start growing my own flowers, so I'd have plenty of petals.

I loved it. I wanted more things to sell.

One day, Mum and Dad were going out for dinner together. Mum smelt so **beautiful**, like the flowers I was using to make my pictures.

She told me that she was wearing perfume, and that perfume was made from flowers. I really wanted to make my own perfume. The next weekend, Mum and I had such a great day trying to make our own perfume. The first perfume we made smelt horrible, like a pair of dirty socks.

My mum and I did some more testing and soon we were able to make some really nice-smelling perfumes. Instead of spraying the perfume on ourselves, we made them into book sprays so people could have nice-smelling notebooks. We have now been selling them to people around the village and at the local market. This means I have been earning money for years.

The great news is that flowers keep on growing so we have a good supply of flowers during the spring and summer. I'm now trying to think of things to make and sell during the winter when the flowers don't grow.

"Wow, that's **AWESOME!**," Boris said. "Maybe I should have stayed awake more at school, then I would have learned all this stuff already."

Actually, this isn't taught in school. I'm not sure why schools don't teach kids about starting their own businesses. Hopefully in the future they will teach kids about starting their own businesses, and becoming what's known as an **ENTREPRENEUR**.

BORIS DREAMS OF STARTING A BUSINESS

"Shall we start a new business together? I'm sure we can come up with something that will make us **GAZILLIONAIRES!**" said Boris excitedly.

"I'm loving the enthusiasm, Boris," replied Gail.

"Before we start creating something, let's meet up again and I will then tell you all about my grandpa's **Three Rules of Wealth**. If you don't know how to look after your money and make it grow, you won't be better off than most people and certainly won't be a gazillionaire. How about we meet up at the Burger Shack again next weekend?"

"Definitely! You really love the **burger shack**, don't you? Next you'll be telling me that you make money from coming here," joked Boris.

Gail didn't answer. She just smiled and made her way home.

Discuss with your Parents, Class, Friends and ...
that Auntie you never talk to

What businesses do you think kids could start?

GRANDPA'S MYSTERY CODE (5)

Answer the question below and put the letter in the corresponding place on page 1 to solve the code.

Which of the below means "someone who starts their own business"?

A: Gold Digger

I: Manager

E: Entrepreneur

Part 3
THE THREE RULES OF
Wealth

THE TRIP TO THE VILLAGE
SAVE THEN SPEND

As Gail approached the **burger shack**, she heard some shouting. It sounded like there was a fight going on.

"Surely not Boris again!" Gail said to herself.

It was Boris. He was fighting two other boys.

Gail was about to go in and tell him that she was never going to speak to him again. Then she noticed something. Boris was fighting with his goon friends.

"You've changed, Boris. You've become such a **LOSER!** You're not even wearing your leather jacket anymore. Next you'll be wearing those dorky t-shirts like your new girlfriend!" shouted one of the goons.

"I don't care what you guys think anymore," blasted Boris.

Gail noticed a scared-looking young boy standing behind Boris. Just then the **burger shack** manager came running over to break up the fight.

"**BORIS!** WHAT'S GOING ON HERE!**" he demanded. Boris' reputation as the village bully had led most people to assume that he was the cause of any trouble.

The young boy quickly stepped forward to tell the manager what had happened. "**Sir**. **Sir**. Those two boys tried to take my lunch money. Boris was sticking up for me. They started the fight, not Boris."

Gail was so surprised by what she'd heard. Did Boris do something nice for someone else? She couldn't have been prouder.

The manager of the Burger Shack was also surprised by Boris' behaviour. "Boris, well done for sticking up for this boy. Maybe I had gotten the wrong impression of you. Next time, try to find a different way to handle the problem without fighting."

Boris started to **BLUSH** at the praise he was getting for sticking up for the boy. He'd never experienced hearing people say such nice things to him, although he was also a bit scared as he had now lost his friends. They would never want to hang out with him after what he'd done.

He then thought about Gail. "Is she a friend or does she just see me as her student?" He'd never had a friend who was a girl before.

Then Gail waved Boris over to the counter so they could order some drinks and fries.

"What you did for that boy was AMAZING! You should feel really proud of yourself. What made you do that kind thing?" asked Gail.

"I really want to know the **Three Rules of Wealth,** so I wanted to show you that I could change. You see, the stories about your grandpa going from having no money to becoming wealthy are so inspiring. I didn't realise someone like me could become rich, I mean, wealthy," replied Boris.

"My grandpa would always say that the most important thing about becoming wealthy is believing that you can become wealthy. Most people don't believe they ever will and therefore never really try," said Gail, smiling. "We'd better go and grab a table so I can tell you all about the **Three Rules of Wealth.**"

They took their trays and sat at a booth. As they sat down, Gail immediately started to explain the first rule.

FIRST RULE OF WEALTH
Keep one out of every ten seeds you receive. (Save)

"When Grandpa was on the island, the best decision he made was to save at least one out of every ten fruits he found. He did the same thing with his money. He would always save at least one dollar out of every ten dollars he received. This became his first rule of wealth," Gail explained.

This first rule meant he always had some money when he needed it.

"THAT SOUNDS REALLY SIMPLE!"

said Boris.

"That's what most people say, but actually it's much harder than you think. There are lots of people trying to get you to spend your money. They will come up with clever ways to make sure you don't end up saving your money," replied Gail. "Remember **RICHIE RACCOON** from Pucha-Pucha? Well, after he decided he was going to start growing his own forest like Grandpa, he struggled to save one of out of every ten seeds he received."

Richie Raccoon's TRIP TO THE VILLAGE

RICHIE RACCOON was excited about planting his own forest. He offered to help Grandpa, or Wealthy Wallaby as he was now known, build a new entrance to his log cabin in exchange for a few seeds.

Grandpa agreed and even told Richie where the best place on Pucha-Pucha was to plant the seeds.

After a hard morning of work, Richie was excited to receive his seeds and start planting his forest. He went to the place Grandpa told him about. As he was walking there, he went through the village that he used to go to every time he found gold. It had been many months since he had last been there.

As he walked through the village, he saw his old friends.

They assumed he was back as he had been lucky enough to find more **GOLD**. He told them that he hadn't found gold for a long time, and that he now had some seeds that he was going to plant, in order to grow his own forest.

As Richie continued walking he was stopped by his friend Baker Bill. In the past, Richie would always go to Bill's bakery to get one of his amazing **Pucha-Pucha Cakes**. Bill was delighted to see Richie and asked him if he'd like a cake. Richie told Bill he didn't have any gold to pay and only had ten seeds which he was going to plant.

Bill said, "I know how much you must miss having one of these cakes. How about you give me three seeds for one piece of cake? You'll still have plenty of seeds left." Richie looked at the cake and couldn't resist. As Bill had said, he'd still have plenty of seeds left.

He enjoyed his cake and said goodbye to Bill.

At the end of the village, there was the clothes shop run by Millie, one of Richie's closest friends.

Again, when Richie used to find gold, he'd always go to Millie's shop to buy new clothes. As he didn't need fancy clothes anymore, he thought there was no harm in popping in and saying hello to Millie.

He told Millie all about not finding gold, meeting Grandpa and how he was going to plant his very own forest. Millie was so happy for him. Then she said, "You're not going planting in those clothes, are you? They'll get ruined and the dirt will be so hard to get out. Do you have any proper clothes for planting your forest?"

"THESE ARE THE ONLY CLOTHES I HAVE LEFT!" replied Richie.

"I happen to have the perfect clothes for you to wear when you plant your forest. You can give me whatever seeds you have. Then when you next get some seeds, you'll be ready to start planting in your new planting clothes and won't have to worry about ruining your nice clothes."

Richie thought about it. He liked the sound of having some new clothes for planting as he pictured himself planting a lot in the future. He thought he could do some more work for Grandpa to get some more seeds, so it wouldn't be much of a delay before he started planting his forest. He tried on his new planting clothes. "These clothes look **AMAZING!!** Thanks Millie." Richie then gave Millie his remaining seven seeds.

The next day, Richie went back to see Grandpa. He asked if he could help with some more jobs to earn seeds to start his forest. Grandpa was shocked to see Richie in his new clothes. "I thought you were going to plant your seeds. Where did you get the new clothes from?" asked Grandpa. Richie explained what had happened at Millie's.

"You need to be careful, Richie," said Grandpa. "You may **NEVER** start growing your forest if you keep giving your seeds away."

Richie assured Wealthy Wallaby that he'd plant his seeds this time.

After a long day of work, Richie collected his seeds from Grandpa and headed off to plant them. As he walked into the village, he said hello to Baker Bill and Millie, but told himself he couldn't go into the bakery or clothes shop as he'd end up giving away his seeds again.

As he was about to leave the village, he bumped into Derick. Derick was wearing an amazing pair of sunglasses. "**WOW!** Those sunglasses look great," said Richie.

"Thanks. Today there is a buy one, get one free **SALE** at the sunglasses store. You should go get your own. Everyone knows you keep losing your sunglasses."

"I don't need any at the moment," said Richie. He went on to explain his story about planting the seeds to grow a forest.

"If you are going to grow a forest, you'll have loads of seeds in the future. This **SALE** is only on for today. By buying two pairs of sunglasses today, you'll be saving yourself from spending more seeds in the future as you'll only need to pay for one pair rather than two!"

Richie thought Derick made a good point. If he bought two pairs now, he'd be saving himself seeds in the future, especially as he kept losing his sunglasses. Like before, he thought he could always earn more seeds from Grandpa later. So

he went to the store to get some before the sale
ended.

Happy with his new sunglasses, Richie went skipping home.

The next day he went back to Grandpa. He knew that Grandpa would ask about his forest and he'd have to say that he had still not planted any seeds.

As soon as Richie arrived, he told Grandpa about how he'd saved by buying the sunglasses on sale. Grandpa asked him, "Before you went to the village, did you think of buying any sunglasses? Or did it come to your mind when you heard they were on **SALE**?"

Richie admitted it was only when he heard about the deal that sunglasses came to his mind.

Grandpa explained to Richie that there would always be people offering deals to make you give away your seeds. It's hard to say no in these situations.

"Here's what you should do,"

Grandpa started. "Instead of going through the village before planting your seeds, take a different route around the side of the village. Then once you have planted some of your seeds, you can walk back through the village. You can use whatever seeds you didn't plant to get the things you want from the village. This way you'll always be planting some of your seeds. **REMEMBER TO PLANT AT LEAST ONE OUT OF EVERY TEN SEEDS BEFORE YOU GO TO THE VILLAGE!**"

This is exactly what Richie did, but it wasn't easy. After a while he got used to going different ways and didn't have to think about going into the village until after planting his seeds.

Soon enough, his seeds grew into trees. The trees started producing more seeds. He kept those seeds in his forest and continued to plant at least one out of every ten seeds he earned helping Grandpa.

GAIL CREATED A HABIT

Gail explained to Boris, "You see, even though most people grow up knowing the first rule of wealth, they end up spending all their money. When they receive money as adults, they continue to spend, and forget to follow the first rule of wealth, especially as there are so many people and companies coming up with clever ways to make us spend all our money."

"BECAUSE WE FORM MONEY HABITS BY THE AGE OF SEVEN," continued Gail, "my parents and grandparents made sure that I saved some of my money from when I first started getting pocket money at the age of four. As I've been saving some money before I go to the shops, I now save money out of habit. This is exactly why they gave me pocket money from such an early age," continued Gail.

"I've never saved any money before! I was just like **RICHIE RACCOON** and just ended up spending any money I was ever given. That's going to change from now on, I'm going to be keeping some of my money!" said Boris

"Great. If you can form the habit of saving a little of the money you receive, you will be on your way to becoming wealthy," replied Gail. "So, now that you know the first rule of wealth is to keep one out of every ten seeds you receive, which is an example of saving, let me tell you the second rule of wealth. The second rule is probably the most exciting, as most people don't know much about it."

Discuss with your Parents, Class, Friends and ...
someone whose name begins with a 'T'

Why do you think is it so important to save some money before you start spending?

GRANDPA'S
MYSTERY CODE (6)

Answer the question below and put the letter in the corresponding place on page 1 to solve the code.

Find the missing word "If you save a little bit of money all the time, it becomes a ____"?

M: Habit

D: Chore

T: Game

the burger shack

INVEST

"To really appreciate the second rule of wealth, you need to think of money as seeds," explained Gail.

"The first rule of wealth is making sure you keep some seeds. The second rule is to make sure you plant those seeds," continued Gail. "You see, if you plant a seed, it will grow into a tree. That tree will grow and start to produce more seeds. You can then take those seeds and plant them which will produce even more trees. This means that from a single seed, you can grow a forest. The more seeds you plant, the bigger your forest will be."

"You can't plant and grow money trees," replied a slightly confused Boris.

"No, you're right. You can't grow money trees, but money can grow like trees as my grandpa told me. You see, if you invest the money you save, it will grow and earn you more money," explained Gail.

"I have no clue what you mean by **'invest your money?'** Is this something only you clever kids know?" asked Boris, doubting if he'd ever be rich.

"When my grandpa told me the second rule of wealth was about 'investing what you save,' I had no idea what investing was either. It's another topic that most schools don't seem to teach. However, my grandpa taught me what investing is by bringing me to this Burger Shack when I was seven years old," said Gail.

SECOND RULE OF WEALTH
Plant the seeds you keep. (Invest)

the burger shack story

When Grandpa took Gail to the Burger Shack, he said, "You see all those people queuing up at the counter to order some food? They will all be giving some of their money to Burger Shack. Each of those people are getting a little bit poorer as they spend their money. However, Burger Shack is getting wealthier as they get the money from people buying those burgers. It's not just those people. There are people all over the world buying food and giving some of their money to Burger Shack. It has restaurants everywhere and is getting wealthier and wealthier."

Grandpa continued, "Now, imagine if you owned **burger shack.** You'd be getting some of that money and you'd be getting wealthier too. That's what investing is all about. If you invest in the STOCK MARKET, you give your money to companies, so that you can own a small piece of them and therefore receive a bit of money from everyone who buys something from them."

He continued to explain that you can invest in many companies. You can own a small part of companies that make computers, toys, cars and movies. This means that every time someone buys a computer, toy, car, or movie you get a small piece of that money.

Grandpa explained that you don't get all the money that **burger shack** makes, as they have to use some of the money from selling their burgers to pay the people who work there. They also must pay for the restaurant building and pay the farmers who provide the beef and potatoes for burgers and fries. Once they pay for these, then they give some money that is left, which is called their PROFIT, to the people who have invested in their company.

Burger Shack uses the money you give them when you invest to create new burgers or open new restaurants. This helps them make more money and they will start giving you more money back, which is called a **DIVIDEND**. The more you have invested in the company, the more you get back from the company.

Remember that investing is like planting a tree. When you invest in Burger Shack think of it like planting a Burger Shack Tree. When they give some money to the people who invested, this is like the Burger Shack Tree producing a seed. The secret to becoming *wealthy* is to plant that seed to grow another tree. This means investing more into Burger Shack. As you have more trees, it means you get more money back each year.

From when I first arrived back home from the island, the money I invested has doubled nearly every ten years. As I've been home from the island for fifty years, each dollar I invested then is now worth over thirty-two dollars.

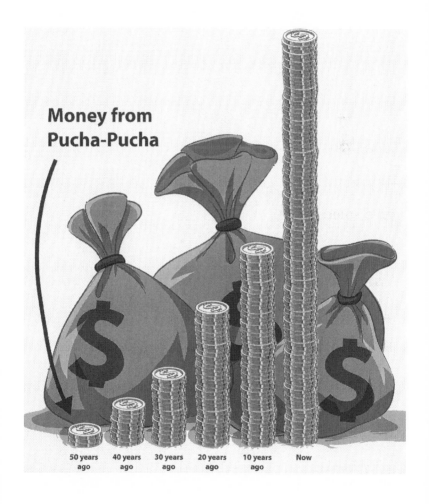

Over the years I've found different ways to earn money. As I invested at least 1 out of every 10 dollars I've ever received, I am now a wealthy man.

The best thing about investing is that the money invested grows without you having to do any extra work.

BORIS WANTS TO INVEST

"You own a piece of **burger shack**, that's so cool! Why doesn't everyone invest their money?" asked Boris.

"Sadly, many people are never taught about investing so they never invest. Or maybe they aren't sure about the best way to invest," replied Gail.

"Please tell me you're going to teach me the best way to invest, **RIGHT?!** questioned Boris.

"Of course. My Grandpa has told me some incredible stories which have taught me all about investing the right way. But first, I want to tell you about the third rule of wealth. This one is really important as there is no point in investing any money if you can't follow this third rule!" said Gail. She then got up to buy an ice cream from the counter, leaving Boris eagerly waiting to learn the third rule of wealth.

Discuss with your Parents, Class, Friends and ...
the quiet kid in school

Why do you think it is important to invest some of your money?

Parents: Setting up an investment account

3-step guide to opening an investment account:

www.bluetreesavings.com/guide

GRANDPA'S
MYSTERY DE (7)

Answer the question below and put the letter in the corresponding place on page 1 to solve the code.

Find the missing word. "The stock market is where you buy ____"?

Y: Burgers

A: Companies

P: Stamps

chapter 8
EIGHT

Richie Raccoon's
RED TREE

DEBT AND GAMBLING

Gail finally returned with the ice creams.

"What took you so long? I was thinking you'd changed your mind and given up on me," said Boris.

Gail smiled "You are so **IMPATIENT**. You'll need to change that if you want to become wealthy. You see, the third rule of wealth is to simply be patient!"

THIRD RULE OF WEALTH
Let your trees grow. (Be patient)

"THAT'S IT? THAT SEEMS SO EASY!" blurted Boris.

"Whilst it seems easy, most people don't follow this rule either. When it comes to money, people really struggle to be patient. They want money straight away and end up getting poorer, not wealthier. Impatient people lose money when investing. They want to see their money grow really quickly and if it seems like it's not growing, they stop investing," explained Gail.

"Also, people who aren't patient with their money try to find shortcuts to get what they want and end up with a lot less than they had before. My grandpa saw this firsthand with his friend Richie Raccoon," continued Gail.

It had been a few weeks since **RICHIE RACCOON** had planted some seeds on Pucha-Pucha. He was so excited about growing his own Fortune Forest, like his friend Wealthy Wallaby, my grandpa.

Each day he would check up on his seeds to see if they had grown into trees. Richie hated waiting. He wanted a forest of trees right now!

Then one day, Richie was walking through the village when he heard some strange noises and cheering. As he continued walking, he noticed some people playing a game. One of them was the famous Exotic Elsa. She was famous, as she had some of the most exotic trees on the whole island.

Richie watched as they were playing. Then one man playing stood up quickly and shouted, **"YES! I'VE WON!!** Elsa, you owe me one of your exotic trees!"

Sure enough, Elsa agreed that she'd give the man one of her exotic trees once she had finished playing.

Richie thought "Wow! This could be the answer to all my problems. If I beat Elsa at this game, I'll get one of her trees! I'll no longer need to wait for my trees to grow!"

They were playing a simple board game where players took turns rolling a die. The first person to get their counter around the board won. They had to make sure they didn't land on the squares which sent them back to the start. The one oddity with the game was that before you rolled you had to say PUCHA exactly ten times in five seconds. If you said it any more or less than ten times you miss your go. (It's harder than you think!)

"Can I play?" Richie asked the group.

"Sure. It costs ten seeds to play," they explained.

Richie had planted all his seeds so didn't have any left. He thought about going home to where he had planted them to dig them up so he could play the game. Then one man playing the game said, "If you don't have any seeds now, you

should visit **MR. CREDIT TREE**.
He will give you some seeds to play. You just need
to pay him back later."

"That sounds great! I can't wait to play,"
replied Richie as he walked to Mr. Credit Tree's
house.

When he got to where Mr. Credit Tree
lived, Richie was amazed by all the beautiful red
trees growing around his house. He'd never seen
trees like that before.

Knock! Knock!

A short stocky man, with square glasses
and only a few hairs on his head answered the
door. "Mr. Credit Tree, please may I borrow ten
seeds?" asked Richie. "Of course! Of course! But
you know you'll have to pay me back." replied Mr.
Credit Tree.

Richie couldn't believe his luck. He said to himself, "I thought I'd have to wait years for my trees to grow. Now, I've got some seeds straight away and I'm going to use these seeds to win Elsa's exotic trees. I'm going to have my own Fortune Forest in no time at all. I'm so glad I don't have to wait!"

As Richie was leaving, he noticed Mr. Credit Tree go outside, plant a few seeds in his garden, and put a sign next to them that said: **"'RICHIE RACCOON: TEN SEEDS.'"** Richie didn't understand what he was doing as he was too excited about playing the game to stop and ask.

Richie practiced saying **PUCHA** ten times quickly all the way back to where they were playing the game. Once he got back, he

RICHIE RACCOON: TEN SEEDS

showed the other players the seeds he'd borrowed.

They pointed to a seat at the table and asked him to sit down as they were about to start a new game.

The game was fun and at the start Richie was doing really well. He was moving his counter around the board and was ahead of the other players. He had the opportunity to roll the die and get to the end. The timer was set and Riche started his go:

PUCHA, PUCHA, **PUCHA**, **PUCHA**, PUCHA, PUCHA, **PUCHA**, **PUCHA**, PUCHA, PUCHA, **PUCHA!**

In his excitement about winning, he said **PUCHA** eleven times and missed his go.

A few moments later, one of the other players got to the end of the board and had won the game. **"I CAN'T BELIEVE THIS!"** Richie cried. He hadn't won any exotic trees. What made it even worse was that he still owed Mr. Credit Tree ten seeds.

He knew that to pay back Mr. Credit Tree, he would have to dig up the seeds he had planted. It was a sad moment for him.

It was going to get even worse still. After he had dug up his ten seeds from his garden, he took them to **MR. CREDIT TREE**. He handed over the seeds and was about to leave when Mr. Credit Tree said, "Thanks for giving me ten seeds. I'll see you when you have the rest of the seeds you owe me!"

"What? I borrowed ten seeds and I have just given you ten seeds, so I don't owe you anymore," snapped Richie.

Mr. Credit Tree led Richie into the garden to a sign that read **"RICHIE RACCOON: TEN SEEDS."** Next to the sign were ten small red trees. "When you borrowed some seeds, I planted some red tree seeds in your name. They have now grown into red trees. You must now pay me back more seeds, as each red tree is worth more than one of your seeds. The bigger the red tree, the more seeds you have to give me. As your trees have grown, you still owe me two seeds," explained Mr. Credit Tree.

"This is so **UNFAIR**. I didn't realise that. I've never seen trees grow so fast," stated Richie.

"I was going to tell you but you ran off so fast. Did you think I'd let you have ten of my seeds for nothing? In fact, if you don't come back with those two seeds within a month, you'll owe me three seeds as the red trees will continue to grow," said Mr. Credit Tree.

Richie couldn't believe it. In his rush to have his own full-grown Fortune Forest, he had lost everything he started with and now still owed more seeds to Mr. Credit Tree.

Richie went to see his friend Wealthy Wallaby to see if he could help. He explained what had happened. He thought his friend would be angry at him for being so silly.

Wealthy Wallaby said, "In order to become wealthy, and have your own **FORTUNE FOREST**, as you call it, you have to be patient. When I first came to Pucha-Pucha, I wanted to get rich quick and got tricked by Shovel Sam. He told me there was gold so I'd buy one of his shovels. I now realise how important it is to be patient and let my trees grow at their own speed. I hope you learned that borrowing seeds and playing games in order to speed things up is more likely to make you worse off than if you'd just waited."

Wealthy Wallaby helped by giving Richie a few jobs to earn some seeds to pay back Mr. Credit Tree before his red trees grew anymore.

Richie worked to earn seeds from that point onwards, planted the seeds, and waited patiently. Whilst it took a long time, he eventually grew his own Fortune Forest and was proud of what he had achieved.

WHAT'S GAMBLING?

"My Grandpa said **RICHIE RACCOON** felt so silly after losing that game. Whilst he thought he could win, he in fact had the same chance as the other players. The winner would be the one who was the luckiest in the game," said Gail.

Gail explained to Boris that people who don't have patience will hear stories of people who win money from playing games and then feel they can also win money. This is called **GAMBLING**.

For everyone who gets lucky winning money by gambling, there are many more who lose.

Grandpa told me to never rely on luck to become wealthy and to never gamble.

WHAT'S DEBT?

"The red trees? What are the red trees in the story?" asked Boris.

Gail explained that lots of people don't have the patience to save up their money to buy what they want. These people then borrow money from people or companies; the money they owe is called **DEBT**.

These people then need to pay back that money over time. Most people don't fully realise that they will have to pay back a lot more than they borrowed, like when Richie had to give back more than the ten seeds he had borrowed as the red trees had grown.

The longer people take to pay back what they borrowed, the more they have to pay.

People who don't have patience are more likely to borrow money or gamble, which makes them poorer. It's also why a lot of people don't invest. They want to see their money grow quickly so give up. Therefore, my grandpa's third rule of wealth is: Let your trees grow. **Be patient.**

Boris was quick to say, "I can see why people struggle with being patient. Whenever I get some money, I spend it all on computer games straight away. My money never lasts long. That's going to change from now on."

"I need to get home," said Gail, "but before I go, do you remember the **Three Rules of Wealth**, Boris?"

"Three Rules of Wealth? I have no clue what you're talking about," replied Boris with a confused look on his face.

Gail was shocked, but before she could say anything Boris said, "JOKE! You should have seen the look on your face," as he laughed and pointed at Gail.

"Of course, I remember the rules. They are:

1. KEEP ONE OUT OF EVERY TEN SEEDS YOU RECEIVE.

2. PLANT THE SEEDS YOU KEEP.

3. LET YOUR TREES GROW."

"Don't do that to me again," replied Gail with a smile. "For a minute I really was going to shout at you for wasting my time. I'm so glad you've been listening!"

"I'm loving the stories. I still can't believe someone like me can become wealthy. Are you sure that it's not just the smart kids who become wealthy?"

"Money isn't about how smart you are. In fact, a lot of smart people don't follow the **Three Rules of Wealth** as they think the rules are too simple for them. I've actually got a t-shirt at home which has one of my grandpa's favourite sayings on it:

"Trust me, if you follow the rules, you will see that you will become wealthy. It will just take time," Gail continued. "Now let's catch up again tomorrow so I can tell you all about the stories my grandpa told me about the missing seeds and the massive storm on **Pucha-Pucha**, which ruined my grandpa's forest. You'll soon know more about investing than most adults!"

Discuss with your Parents, Class, Friends and ...
your favourite soft toy

Why do you think being patient is so important when it comes to money?

GRANDPA'S MYSTERY CODE (8)

Answer the question below and put the letter in the corresponding place on page 1 to solve the code.

Find the missing word "In order to avoid gambling, debt and scams you need to be ___"?

Y: Patient

R: Lucky

T: Rich

Part 4

MAKING MONEY

Grow

THE MISSING SEEDS TAX

Gail turned up at the Burger Shack to meet Boris, but he was nowhere to be found. She waited a little longer but still no Boris.

"He seemed so keen to learn! Why has he changed his mind?" Gail thought to herself.

Gail knew where he lived so she decided to go and look for Boris. As she approached his house, she saw Boris' mum outside.

"Hello Mrs. Duckworth, is Boris home?" asked Gail.

"Yes, but he's **GROUNDED!** He was trying to tell us some nonsense about how he would become wealthy and how we are not looking after our money. I bet you wouldn't speak to your parents like that, would you?" said Mrs. Duckworth.

Gail felt so guilty for getting Boris into trouble.

"Mrs. Duckworth, my name is Gail Fitzgerald. I think this is all my fault. I've been telling Boris all about my grandpa, Jack Fitzgerald. It seems that he has gotten a little over-excited. I really believe he was trying to help you, but his approach has come across as rude," said Gail.

"You're the granddaughter of the **MILLIONAIRE JACK FITZGERALD** and you're friends with my Boris?" said Mrs. Duckworth in complete shock.

"Yes. We are good friends, and we might even start a business together," replied Gail.

"I don't know what to say. You're not like any of his other friends. I hope you're not trying to put ideas in his head. **We are not like your family**; we don't have much money. Boris also isn't doing that well in school so I don't want you getting his hopes up that he can become rich. He never will! Not unless he gets really lucky and wins the lottery!" said Mrs. Duckworth.

"My grandpa's family had little money when he was growing up. I've been fortunate that my grandpa has been teaching me about money and now I'm trying to help Boris. He's keen to learn. Please, will you let me see him? I promise not to get his hopes up and I'll make sure he doesn't speak to you like he did again," said Gail.

"I suppose I'll allow it, but he's still not allowed to leave the house. You'll have to speak to him inside," said Mrs. Duckworth.

Gail walked into the house as Mrs. Duckworth shouted for Boris to come out of his bedroom. "BORIS!"

Gail looked around and noticed they had a nice house. They had a big TV, a nice leather sofa, and plenty of holiday photos scattered around. "I thought they didn't have any money," she said to herself.

Boris came down from his bedroom. He looked angry.

"Sorry I couldn't meet you. My mum is **evil.** I tried to help her, and she grounded me!" said Boris.

"Don't worry about it, Boris. You shouldn't say your mum is evil. I'm sure she loves you very much. I heard you started telling her that she was using her money all wrong," said Gail.

"My parents aren't following any of the **Three Rules of Wealth** you told me about. You can see that they earn a good amount of money, but they spend it all on stuff. I was trying to tell them that they need to change. Instead of thanking me, they grounded me. It's so unfair," said Boris.

"People don't like to be told they are doing something wrong. When your parents were growing up, they were probably never taught about money. So, when you told your parents they aren't following the rules, they probably found it upsetting. One of the best things to do is to show them that you can manage money and then help them. Start earning some money, save some of it and then ask them to set up an investment account so you can invest it," replied Gail.

"I guess so . . . I want them to learn about money so they will **stop arguing** over money," said Boris.

"Do you have time to hear what my grandpa told me about how to invest?" asked Gail.

"You know I do," said Boris as he started to smile again. "I've already been thinking about all the different companies I want to own!"

Gail explained that before you consider what companies to own, you first need to make sure you invest in a way which allows you to keep as much of your money as possible.

Gail then told Boris the story of when Grandpa planted seeds in different places around Pucha-Pucha.

THE MISSING SEEDS STORY

When Grandpa was on the island of Pucha-Pucha he would plant seeds in two different parts of the island. After a while he noticed that one part of the island had many more trees growing compared to the other part.

He couldn't work out why this was the case. He was planting the same number of seeds, the same type of seeds and planting them at a similar time.

At first, he thought it was because the weather might be slightly different, as the two parts of the island were quite far apart. However, it didn't seem that the weather was different enough that it would produce such different results.

Grandpa was really confused. He sat down to think about what else he could do to see the difference. As he looked up at his trees, he was mesmerised by the birds' song in the trees.

♪ TWEET ♪ TWEET
♪ TWEET ♪

It was simply a beautiful song. He listened for hours.

The next day, Grandpa continued to try and find out why the trees were growing differently. He looked at the soil, but it all seemed the same. Then he noticed that there were bumps in the soil on one part of the island. He went to have a look and noticed that some of the seeds he had planted had **DISAPPEARED**. Someone has been taking Grandpa's seeds.

Grandpa was so angry. He went around the island seeing if anyone knew who had been taking his seeds. He had no luck. He even hid behind trees to see if he could spot someone coming into the forest and catch them taking his seeds. Days went past, and he didn't see anyone.

One day he sat down beside a tree to think. As he sat, he tried to listen out for the birds again. However, he couldn't hear them. **"WHERE HAVE ALL THE BIRDS GONE?"** thought Grandpa. It was then that he realised that the last time he heard the birds he was sitting in the part of the island where there weren't as many trees growing. "It must be the

birds!" shouted Grandpa. "They must be taking my seeds!"

He got up and ran over to the other part of the forest where he'd been sitting before.

As he had thought, he could hear the birds singing again. Sure enough, as he looked closer, he could see the birds eating some of the seeds from his trees.

As the **birds** weren't eating the seeds in the other part of the island, it meant more trees could grow.

As he'd never seen the birds before, he went back to look at them more closely. At first, he tried to think of ways to get rid of them—like making loud noises. But then he saw what the birds were doing.

Grandpa was fascinated to discover that the birds were taking the seeds to help other animals in the forest. They weren't only taking seeds from his forest. They were taking them from lots of different places.

GRANDPA PLANTED MORE SEEDS on the side of the island where there weren't any birds. Soon he was able to grow many more trees than he had been growing before.

WHAT'S TAX?

Gail was quick to tell Boris that this story was her grandpa's way of teaching her about TAX. Grandpa would always refer to tax as the **MONeY BiRDS**.

Gail explained that the government requires people to pay tax on the money they make and what they own. The government uses that money to help build schools and roads and to help those in need. She said it was a bit like the Money Birds who were helping the other animals.

Whilst the government wants you to pay tax, the government also wants people to save their money, so they allow you to save and invest some money in places you don't have to pay tax.

When you plant your seeds, it's best to plant them where there are no Money Birds. The same is true when it comes to investing. When you start to invest, make sure you learn to invest in places where the government allows you to keep all your money and you don't have to pay tax. This means your money will grow to its full potential.

"**GREAT!** I'll make sure to invest where there are no Money Birds, I mean, tax," said Boris.

Gail smiled. "I knew you'd find my grandpa's use of trees and Money Birds easy to remember! I've got a few more of his forest stories to tell you to help make understanding investing super easy. Let me tell you about the massive storm that hit Pucha-Pucha. It almost ruined everything Grandpa had been building."

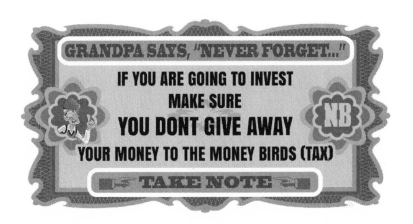

Discuss with your Parents, Class, Friends and ...
a famous pop star

Do you think tax is a good thing or bad thing and why?

GRANDPA'S
MYSTERY  DE (9)

Answer the question below and put the letter in the corresponding place on page 1 to solve the code.

Which of the below means "Money taken by the government to pay for schools, roads, hospitals and much more"?

W: Pension

M: Charity

R: Tax

RISK

"Gail, can I show you the list of companies I want to invest in? As I used to spend all my money on computer games, I want to invest in some computer game companies. And of course, Burger Shack ..." Boris was about to go on listing companies before Gail stopped him.

"Like you, I got really excited about which companies I wanted to invest my money into. I listed the names of toy companies and my favourite restaurant chains. However, my grandpa's story about the **STORM** that hit Pucha-Pucha completely changed my thinking about how I invest."

Everyone on Pucha-Pucha was fascinated by a local farmer named Kai. He had grown a forest of a relatively unknown tree called the Kingsley tree. His Kingsley trees had grown extremely fast over one year and produced more fruits than any other type of tree on the island.

People from all over came to buy the seeds from Kingsley Kai, as he was now known. They all wanted to grow their own Kingsley trees. People kept telling Grandpa that they had witnessed Kingsley Kai's trees growing and that he should buy some Kingsley seeds.

Grandpa didn't understand why the Kingsley trees were going so fast, He decided to buy some seeds from Kingsley Kai, but only a few just in case it was another scam.

Other people cut down many slower growing trees to replace them with Kingsley trees. **"WE'RE GOING TO HAVE THE BIGGEST TREES, LIKE KAI!"** they'd all say.

For days and weeks after, the Kingsley trees kept growing much quicker than the other types of trees on the island. Then, it all changed. The largest storm ever to hit the island came.

SMASH! CRASH! CRACK!

The storm caused tremendous damage. Most of the trees were either broken or torn down completely. Houses were destroyed. The fruits from the trees flew off and ended up sinking deep into the sea.

After all that time growing his forest, Grandpa was devastated. His forest was now in ruins.

Once the storm was over, he looked to see what was left of his forest. Many of the trees were badly damaged. He then went to look for his Kingsley trees. They were nowhere to be seen. The storm had completely pulled them out of the ground and blown them out to sea.

Grandpa felt so lucky he hadn't been one of those that had cut down all their trees to replace them with Kingsley trees. Kingsley Kai and many

others had lost everything they had planted.

One lesson that Grandpa took from the storm was that he had no idea why some trees were more broken than others. He was glad he had lots of different types of trees. When he started planting again after the storm, he planted as many different types of seeds as he could find.

He was so thankful he did this as something amazing happened. One type of tree, called the **RABBIT-CLAW** tree, grew rapidly. Before the storm it was a regular tree and never grew that quickly. Now it was growing more quickly and producing lots of fruits for Grandpa to sell. He thought about planting many more Rabbit-Claw trees, but he remembered what had happened to Kai's Kingsley trees. What if he planted lots of Rabbit-Claw trees and something like that happened to them? "I'd rather have small amounts of many different trees than have a lot of one type of tree," said Grandpa.

Grandpa's forest kept growing and after a couple of years, it was much bigger than it had been before the storm.

GAIL EXPLAINS RISK

"So that's why you are wearing that t-shirt today!" said Boris, pointing to Gail's t-shirt which had **"AFTER A STORM, A TREE WILL GROW BACK STRONGER"** written on it.

"Well spotted!" said Gail with a smile.

Gail then began to tell Boris that one important thing about investing is that there are times when there are storms. This means there are times when the money you invest doesn't keep growing. In fact, sometimes your money can even be less than you started with—like when the trees were broken in the **STORM**.

Gail explained that when her parents first started helping her invest, a virus was making people all around the world ill. To stop the virus people were told to stay at home. As people stayed at home, they weren't spending their money in the different companies she had invested in. **burger shack** wasn't making as much money because people couldn't go out and buy burgers. This meant the money she had invested in Burger Shack was worth less than before.

"I was really upset that I had lost money investing, but my grandpa told me that I hadn't lost any money. 'You only lose money if you give up and stop investing. If you don't give up, it will recover, like a tree will regrow after a storm.'

That's exactly what had happened. After the virus was controlled, people were allowed out of their homes, they went back to spending their money and companies, like **burger shack**,

THE STOCK MARKET HAS ALWAYS GROWN DESPITE THE STORMS

started making more money. I was so happy I didn't stop investing during the virus!"

"Which companies did you invest in, Gail?" asked Boris.

"You see, whilst I wanted to only invest in the few companies on my list, those companies could go bust and I'd lose all my money—like Kai's Kingsley trees disappearing in the storm. So, I invested in thousands of different companies," said Gail.

"Could go **BUST**, what does that mean?" asked Boris.

BLOCKBUSTER VIDEO GOES BUST

Gail told Boris a real-life story about a company called Blockbuster Video. "Blockbuster Video was a place like a library, but instead of books, people borrowed movies. People would pay a small amount for a movie and would be given a small box which contained the movie; they called it a video. They would then put this video in a machine to watch the movie on their TV.

"No way! Our parents really had it hard when they were younger. Imagine not being able to just pick a movie straight from the TV," said Boris.

"Exactly!" replied Gail as she told Boris that as we can now pick movies straight from our TV, no one needed to go to Blockbuster anymore. Blockbuster stopped making money and went out of business, or '**BUST**' as they call it. People who invested in Blockbuster lost money."

Whilst someone might tell you a certain company will do better than another, no one really knows, just like no one knew Grandpa's

Rabbit-Claw trees would do well or Kai's Kingsley trees would disappear. It's best to invest a little bit in many different companies. "This is called **DIVERSIFICATION**," said Gail.

"Not sure I'll be able to invest into thousands of companies. I don't have as much money as you, " stated Boris.

"Actually, you can do the same as me, even with small amounts of money. My parents give the money I want to invest to an investment company. They invest our money into thousands of companies around the world for us through what is called an **INVESTMENT FUND**. Each month we invest more into this Investment Fund. Like Grandpa's forest, we now have lots of different types of trees growing."

"THAT SOUNDS EASY!" said Boris, realising that he had said the same thing about most of the different money topics he had learned.

"I know! Most people think investing is hard, but it's a lot easier if you don't have to worry about which companies to pick. Invest in an investment fund which picks them all and you'll do better than most people," said Gail. "Now, let me tell you the story my grandpa told me about Mr. Lazy's Trees!"

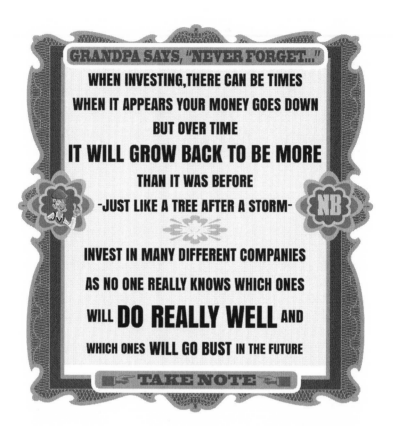

Discuss with your Parents, Class, Friends and ...
Siri, Alexa or google

Why do some companies do well and others not?

GRANDPA'S
MYSTERY  CODE (10)

Answer the question below and put the letter in the corresponding place on page 1 to solve the code.

Find the missing word. "Investing in lots of companies in case one company goes bust is called ____"?

O: Diversification

I: Risk

U: Return

MR LAZY'S TREES

STRATEGY

Gail was about to tell Boris another one of Grandpa's amazing tales when Boris noticed something. "Your headphones are awesome! Are they new?" he asked.

"Yes. I've been saving up for them for a while. I was so excited when I finally had enough money to buy them," replied Gail.

"Why didn't you use the money you've invested to buy them earlier?" asked Boris.

"The money I invested is for the long-term and to grow. *I WON'T TOUCH THAT MONEY* until I'm much older—like Grandpa never cut down his trees until his forest was very large," said Gail.

Gail continued, "Remember, when I earn money, I save at least one out of every ten dollars (**THE FIRST RULE OF WEALTH**), so I still have plenty left for spending or helping others. If this isn't enough to buy what I want, then I wait a few weeks until I do. This helps me learn to be patient (**THE THIRD RULE OF WEALTH**)."

"Good point. I still need to learn to be patient. Anyway, you were going to tell me about MR LAZY. He sounds like my kind of guy," joked Boris.

MR LAZY'S TREES STORY

After growing their own forests for a number of years, Grandpa and **RICHIE RACCOON** decided they didn't want their forest to be the same as everyone else's. They wanted to have the biggest trees they could possibly grow.

The problem was, they didn't know how to make their trees grow bigger and stronger. Should they cut off the broken branches? Should they put any special food in the soil? Should they check on their trees every day?

Grandpa and Richie decided to go and find the biggest trees on the island. They would then find the people who grew those trees to ask what they did to make their trees grow tall.

After searching for many days, they found a group of very **IMPRESSIVE TREES**. They were significantly bigger than all those around them. As they stood admiring the trees, a man walking his dog passed by. "Excuse me, do you know who these trees belong to?" Richie asked.

The man replied, "They belonged to Mr. Robinson. Sadly, he passed away over seven years ago!"

Grandpa and Richie were disappointed not to be able to find out Mr. Robinson's secrets. They decided to go and find other large trees.

After a few more days they came across another group of large trees. They weren't as big as the late Mr. Robinson's trees, but they were impressive. Again, as they admired the trees, they stopped a passer-by to ask who the trees belonged to. The passer-by said he believed they belonged to Ms. Ridley, who owned the village tea shop. They went to the shop to speak with Ms. Ridley.

They ordered a hot pot of tea and a piece of cake. As Ms. Ridley handed them their drinks and cakes, they asked her about her trees.

"MY TREES? WHAT TREES?"

replied Ms. Ridley.

"We were told the trees on the hill belong to you!" Grandpa explained.

"Oh yes, I completely forgot. I planted those trees many years ago. Why do you want to talk to me about those trees?" she asked.

They explained that they wanted to know her secrets, but given she didn't even remember she had the trees, they would not learn much. They paid her for the drink and cake and left.

Although the first two people were of no help, they were determined to continue their search to find the secrets to growing the **LARGEST TREES**.

As they continued their search, they came across the most impressive set of trees they had ever seen. They both hoped they would be able to find the owner of the trees and learn his or her secrets.

As they looked for people to ask about who owned the trees, they went to the village. The local police officer informed them the trees belonged to Mr. Lazy who lived a few doors from where they were standing. Excited to hopefully find the secrets to growing the largest trees, they ran to Mr. Lazy's house.

They knocked on the door, but there was no answer. They tried again but no answer. They were going to give up, but knocked one last time. They heard, **"WHAT DO YOU WANT?"** from the garden at the back of the house.

"We want to ask you about your trees!" replied the friends.

"OK, let yourselves in, I'm in the garden. I don't want to get out of my hammock!"

Grandpa and Richie walked through the house and into the garden. "We are so pleased to meet you, Mr. Lazy!"

"You know my name isn't MR LAZY. That's what people in the village call me!"

"**Sorry**. We want to ask you about your secrets to how you grew your trees so big. Would you be happy to share with us so we can grow our trees as big as yours?"

"OK, but this will be quick," replied Mr. Lazy. "When I started growing my trees many years ago, I planned to look after them as best I could. I even bought special tree food as I saw that's what Ms. Patel was giving to her trees. However, when I was about to give the food to my trees, I couldn't find my shoes. By the time I found my shoes I had completely forgotten about the trees."

"Then, a few months later, there were rumours of a large storm coming. Some people in the village tried to protect their trees by cutting some of the tree branches off so their trees would be stronger. I was going to do the same, but I was in the middle of a great sleep and it was cold outside. It turned out the storm never came so my trees were fine."

"What about when the big storms have hit the island? Did you do anything then?" asked Grandpa.

"Nope. I was going to chop down the broken branches, but I couldn't find my axe, so I just stayed at home. However, it was a good thing I didn't as the trees grew back bigger and stronger."

Grandpa was shocked. "Are you telling us that whilst everyone around you was going out to look after their trees, you stayed at home and did nothing the whole time?!"

"YEP, THAT'S WHAT I DID!"

The two friends were so angry that Mr. Lazy had wasted their time.

As they walked to find other big trees, Richie said, "We aren't having much luck at all! No one we've spoken to has provided us with any secrets to growing large trees. Essentially, they've all done absolutely nothing!"

"THAT'S IT!" exclaimed Grandpa. "The secret to growing the biggest trees is to do nothing! We've been looking for actions to take, but those who did nothing and left their trees alone now have the biggest trees. They do nothing no matter if a storm is coming or not. That's what we should do with our trees! **ABSOLUTELY NOTHING!"**

This is what they did and how they grew their forest. Even when the storms were blowing the tops off their trees, they remembered the people they had met and did nothing. They sat back and soon enough their trees kept getting broken in the storms, but grew back bigger and stronger.

"Who would have guessed the best strategy is also the simplest!" said Richie.

INVESTING MISTAKES PEOPLE MAKE

"The truth is that if you invest in an investment fund and do nothing, you'll end up better off than most people who invest. You see, most people who invest try to guess when a storm is coming or guess which companies will grow the quickest. The more they guess, the less their investments are likely to grow. The hard part is doing nothing when the stock market falls, just like it is hard to do nothing when seeing your trees damaged in a **STORM**," explained Gail.

"Who would have guessed that my natural ability to be lazy would help me make money!" Boris said with a smile.

Then Gail and Boris noticed Boris' mum was standing behind them.

Boris was initially worried about what she had heard, as he was sure that she'd never let him invest money.

"I've been listening to your stories, Gail. **THEY ARE AMAZING**. I knew nothing about investing. I have only ever heard about people losing money from investing. But you have made it seem so simple," she continued. "Boris, if you do earn some money, then I'm more than happy to spend some time setting up an investment account so you can invest and grow your money."

Boris was in shock! **"REALLY?** You'd set up an investment account so I can invest some money?"

"Yes, I will. Also, Boris, I'm sorry for grounding you. You were trying to help, but as you know, your father and I don't like to think about money. As we were never taught about money, we never seem to have enough, which makes us upset. That is why I didn't want to talk about it when you tried to help us yesterday. Maybe we could learn something from you, Gail and, your grandpa. I'm going to talk to your father, Boris, as we should probably look to save some of our own money and start investing it too. I thought you had to be really smart to invest.

Now I realise it's not about how smart you are, it's about how patient you are!"

Gail was delighted by what she had just heard from Boris' mum. But then she said something which worried Gail.

Discuss with your Parents, Class, Friends and ...
Warren Buffett (if you don't know who he is, google him)

Why do you think people find it hard to 'do nothing' when they invest their money?

Parents: If you wish to set up an investment account for your kids, here is a simple guide:

www.bluetreesavings.com/guide

GRANDPA'S
MYSTERY CODE (11)

Answer the question below and put the letter in the corresponding place on page 1 to solve the code.

Find the missing word. "Once you plant your seeds, or invest, the best thing to do is ____"?

I: Chop down the trees as soon as they grow.

E: Dig up the seeds and move them somewhere else.

Y: Leave your trees alone.

THE COMPETITION

A HOME IS NOT AN ASSET

Boris' mum said, "If we invest, we might finally have enough money to buy a big house like the Jones' down the road!"

Gail remembered a story about Tiny Tina that her grandpa had told her. It was a story that meant Boris' mum's wish to move to a bigger house might not be the best idea. She wanted to share this story with Boris' mum but didn't want to upset her.

Gail thought for a while and then said, "Mrs. Duckworth, you have a lovely home at the moment. I think it's great you have enjoyed my grandpa's stories about investing. **Please may I tell you one more?** It's about someone who wanted the same thing as you but did something else and is now thrilled."

"Of course, I'd love to hear another one of your grandpa's stories. I need to learn as much as possible!" replied Mrs. Duckworth.

Gail went on to tell Boris and his mum all about Tiny Tina and the Best Tree Competition.

There was once a lady called Tiny Tina. She had recently started to grow her own tree. It was a beautiful Purple Tree. The great thing about Purple Trees is they are big enough to live in. This makes them special and different from all the other trees on the island.

One day, Tiny Tina saw a sign saying:

She was keen to enter the competition as she was so proud of the Purple Tree she had been growing.

On competition day, the competitors walked around the island to see all the different types of trees entered. There was Simple Susan with her collection of Blue Trees. There was Tree Man Tony with his Yellow Trees. There were also the Rental Robinsons with their own Purple Trees.

The judges looked at all the trees and made their decision. Sadly, Tiny Tina didn't win the competition. In fact, she came in **last place**.

Whilst Tiny Tina was sad, she felt she didn't win as she was new to the competition and her tree wasn't as big as the others. She told herself she'd make some changes to her tree, so she'd be more successful next year.

Over the following year Tiny Tina's Purple Tree grew bigger. She'd even tidied up some of the broken branches. She **Loved** how her Purple Tree was looking now. She felt her tree could now do really well in the competition. For her, she didn't want to live anywhere else other than in her Purple Tree.

Tiny Tina turned up and saw all the other competitors from last year. Like her tree, their trees had also grown.

The judges went around looking at all the trees. They asked Tiny Tina, "Do you live in your tree?"

"YES, I DO!" replied Tiny Tina proudly. She waited for the results and was getting excited about potentially winning a prize.

The judges had made their decision. Sadly, Tiny Tina's Purple Tree came in last again! **"HOW CAN THIS BE?"** thought Tiny Tina. "I'm not going to give up!"

Over the next year, Tiny Tina's Purple Tree continued to grow. She read lots of magazines which showed her how to make trees even more beautiful. She traded some of her fruits she had been storing for the winter to make a beautiful garden around the bottom of her tree. The garden had a nice fence and a small pond.

Again, she turned up at the competition. Like last year, the other trees had also grown. However, they didn't have a beautiful garden around their tree like Tiny Tina. She felt she was going to do really well.

The judges came around and again asked, "Are you still living in your tree?"

"Yes, I love it and wouldn't want to live anywhere else!" replied Tiny Tina.

The results came in and to her surprise she was .... **Last again!!**

Tiny Tina was so sad. She didn't know why she kept coming in last. She went to find one judge to find out why she was last again despite giving away all her fruits to build her beautiful garden around her tree.

The judge explained, "Whilst your **PURPLE TREE** is big and beautiful, in fact one of the most beautiful trees in the competition, we aren't judging the trees on how big or beautiful they are. We are judging the trees on the number of fruits they produce. You see, whilst your tree is beautiful, as you are living in your tree it's not producing any fruits. In fact, as you gave away fruits to build your garden, you scored less points than last year. All the other trees in the competition have grown and produced fruits," the judge explained.

"What about the Rental Robinsons with their Purple Trees?" asked Tiny Tina.

"They don't live in their Purple Trees. They let other people live in their trees who give the

Rental Robinsons fruits in exchange. So, their Purple Trees are producing many fruits," said the judge.

Tiny Tina was **disappointed**; she didn't realise the competition was not about how big or beautiful her Purple Tree was. She then realised how many fruits it had taken her to make her tree so beautiful.

Tiny Tina initially thought about no longer living in her Purple Tree so her tree would start producing fruits. However, she loved her home and didn't want to leave.

In the end, Tiny Tina decided she was going to stay in her beautiful Purple Tree; it was her home after all. Instead, she said to herself, "From now on I'm not going to use any more fruits to make my Purple Tree any better. IT'S FINE JUST THE WAY IT IS!"

She then started planting some of the seeds from the fruits she had left to grow different tree types. She grew a few Blue Trees. They grew and grew over the next couple of years. She then entered the 'Best Tree Competition' with her Blue Trees and won the prize for:

MOST FRUITS FROM A NEW TREE!

Now Tiny Tina has a nice Purple Tree to live in and many other trees which are producing fruits. She helps other people on the island understand the competition rules before they decide to use all their fruits on finding a big Purple Tree to live in.

GAIL EXPLAINS THAT A HOME IS NOT AN ASSET

"I wanted to tell you this story, Mrs. Duckworth, as you mentioned that you wanted to buy a bigger house. Like Tiny Tina in the story, most people believe a bigger house is a sign of wealth, but a bigger house costs more and therefore is taking money out of your pocket," said Gail.

"**I'VE NEVER THOUGHT ABOUT THAT**. Maybe I should speak with Mr. Duckworth. If we stayed in this house and invested some money in the stock market, we could retire early and travel the world," replied Mrs. Duckworth.

"That sounds like a great idea. If you invest some money, you are buying ASSETS which put money into your pocket over time," said Gail.

"Thank you so much for teaching Boris and me, about money. I wish I had been taught about this when I was younger!" said Mrs. Duckworth.

"Will I see you again soon? I've got a great idea for a new business we can work on together," said Boris.

"Of course. Let's meet at the Donkey Sanctuary next Saturday," replied Gail.

"Why the Donkey Sanctuary?" asked Boris, "Cool kids like me don't want to be seen at a lame DONKEY SANCTUARY!"

"Remember when my grandpa first arrived on Pucha-Pucha and he met Shovel Sam who tricked him into buying a shovel? Well, I want to tell you a story about what happened to him. The Donkey Sanctuary is a great place to tell you this story. You'll see why next weekend," said Gail as she picked up her bag to leave.

Discuss with your Parents, Class, Friends and ...
the last person you spoke to on the phone

Why do think it's so important not to spend all your money on your home when you are older?

GRANDPA'S MYSTERY  CODE (12)

Answer the question below and put the letter in the corresponding place on page 1 to solve the code.

Find the missing word "____ puts money into your pocket over time"?

Y: Debt

R: New furniture

N: An asset

Part 5

HELPING

Others

SHOVEL SAM
AND THE
Happy Fairies
CHARITY

Boris was so excited to see Gail again. He had come up with an idea for a new business they could start and was keen to share it with her. He also had some other exciting news for her.

When he saw Gail waiting at the Donkey Sanctuary entrance, he started to run so he could share his news. "You'll never guess what happened! My parents have set up an investment account. I can now start investing any money I save! Gazillionaire, here I come," said Boris excitedly.

"That's great! You'll be following the **Three Rules of Wealth** and growing your own Fortune Forest before you know it!" said Gail.

"Why are we here?" asked Boris. Just as he said that he looked up and saw the big sign above the entrance:

"Is this your grandpa's Donkey Sanctuary?" Boris asked quickly before Gail could answer his earlier question.

"It's not his. They named it after my grandparents as they have donated money to help the sanctuary over many years."

"I've heard you and your family give money away. Seems stupid to me. Shouldn't you be keeping your money, so you become wealthier?" asked Boris.

"I used to think the same thing, then one day my grandpa told me a story about when Richie Raccoon met his friend Shovel Sam on Pucha-Pucha. After hearing this story, I wanted to start using some of my money to help others, like my parents and grandparents do," said Gail.

SHOVEL SAM AND THE HAPPY FAIRIES

Many years after learning the importance of growing a Fortune Forest, **RICHIE RACCOON** had finally grown his own. He was so happy that he could grow his fruits to sell at the market to make some money and didn't have to spend his days digging for gold.

Now that Richie had money, he felt he wanted to buy some nice clothes, like when he used to find gold on the island.

He went to Millie's clothing store. While he was trying on clothes, **SHOVEL SAM** came in.

Richie and Sam used to be best friends. For many years, they were the richest men on the island. They would always wear the nicest clothes and eat the best food. Everyone wanted to be as rich as them. That was before Richie couldn't find any more gold and lost everything he had.

"It's so great to see you again Richie," said Sam. "I love those clothes you are trying on! I'm so glad you are rich again. Why don't we meet up tonight for dinner at that expensive restaurant we used to go to all the time?"

Richie thought back to when he used to go to that restaurant and eat some of the **tastiest food**. He thought it wouldn't hurt to go there again as he now had some money from selling his fruits.

"OK—it would be nice to go back there. I'll see you tonight," said Richie as he paid for his new clothes and left the shop.

That night, he put on his new clothes and walked to the village where the restaurant was.

"Wow, **those new shoes look amazing.** I wish I could afford a pair of shoes like that," said Baker Bill as Richie walked past the bakery.

"Hi Richie, I that jacket you are wearing. It looks so nice," said one of the ladies he knew in the village.

Richie loved the feeling of everyone complimenting his new clothes. It was like the old days when he had found loads of gold.

He got to the restaurant and saw Sam sitting at the table. They talked about all the fun they used to have. They ate one of the best meals Richie had had in years.

"COME ON, let's take a walk through the village so everyone can see our new clothes. I love that feeling of everyone admiring me. They

all wish they could have what we have," said Sam.

They walked around the village, and everyone paid them compliments. However, for Richie, something didn't feel right. He didn't want to **SHOW OFF**. He wanted to stop and share the stories he had learned from Grandpa so they could become wealthy too. That night Richie didn't sleep well at all.

The next day, Sam came to Richie's house. But Richie wasn't there. Sam was about to leave when he saw Richie coming back.

"Hi Sam. How are you? I've just been helping some people in the village repair their roofs as they were damaged in the recent storm."

"No worries. I was looking at your house. **It's soooo SMALL.** When are you going to move to a big house like you used to live in?"

"I like this house. I don't need a bigger one," replied Richie.

"OK, at least you have money to buy nice clothes and eat nice meals. Shall we go to the shop again today and then go for dinner as we had so much fun last night?" said Sam.

"Not tonight, Sam. I enjoyed our meal but today I decided to use my money to help people in the village fix their roofs," replied Richie.

"REALLY!?" Why are you helping them? You've worked hard for your money; you should spend that money on yourself!" said Sam.

"That's what I used to think. Now I want to help others. Whilst it's nice to hear compliments about my nice new clothes, it doesn't feel as nice as the feeling I get from helping others. I'm going to spend the afternoon at the school teaching the kids about how to grow their own forest. I want them all to grow something to sell at the market so they can buy nice things and help others," said Richie.

"You can come with me if you'd like, Sam. I think you might want to hear what I've learned from my friend *Wealthy Wallaby*. When people realise there is no more gold left on this island, then you won't have anyone to buy your shovels and won't be rich for much longer," Richie explained to Sam.

Sam went to hear the stories Richie told the school kids. It really got him thinking. He felt he now needed to start growing his own forest. He didn't want to continue tricking people into believing there was gold on the island so he could sell them shovels.

After some discussion, he decided he'd only sell his shovels to the farmers and people on the

island who were trying to grow their own forests. As he knew some people couldn't afford his shovels, he decided to give one shovel out of every ten to someone who couldn't afford one.

Richie and Sam met up again after a few months. "It feels **AMAZING** helping all these people to grow their own forests. They are also taking the time to teach me how best to grow my forest. I didn't realise people were so kind! Also, I'm now sleeping better than ever before," said Sam.

"My friend told me when you help others then the **Happy Fairies** come out and look after you. They make you feel better and, as you mentioned, help you sleep better," said Richie.

One day a boy came up to Sam and Richie and said, "Years ago, I wanted to have all the money, clothes and food like you had. Now I want to help as many people as you are helping."

"That's the best compliment I have ever received!" said Sam to the boy.

GAIL EXPLAINS THE BENEFITS OF CHARITY

"I love giving some money to the Donkey Sanctuary. I also like spending time here too as I'm helping these poor animals. Without people helping them, they wouldn't have enough food or a nice place to live," explained Gail.

Gail continued, "I also feel really good about myself for helping others. You see, the **Happy Fairies** in the story were Grandpa's way of telling Richie about what happens to your body when you are kind to others. When you do something nice for other people, your body produces something inside you which makes you feel good. It's called oxytocin **(OX-SUH-TOW-SIN).** It not only makes you feel good, but it can also actually make you feel better and sleep better. So, giving to charity not only helps other people, but it also actually helps you as well!"

"Wow! I spend so much time playing computer games whilst you are doing these amazing things. I don't have much money to give to charity at the moment, but I'd be keen to come here with you in the future to help-especially as some of the people here are cooler than I thought. They aren't all dorks," said Boris, now knowing Gail actually liked being a dork.

"That's great. Now, please tell me your business plan. I'm really excited to hear about it," said Gail.

Discuss with your Parents, Class, Friends and ...
the kindest person you know

What charity would you help and why?

GRANDPA'S
MYSTERY  DE (13)

Answer the question below and put the letter in the corresponding place on page 1 to solve the code.

"Who did Grandpa say comes when we give to charity?"

O: The Red Tree Squirrels

I: The Money Birds

V: The Happy Fairies

Grandpa's hIGh ChAIRS
STARTING A BUSINESS

"Before I tell you my business plan, check out this t-shirt I got made." Boris lifted his jumper to show the t-shirt he was wearing.

Gail couldn't believe it. It was just like the t-shirt she wore. "I've turned you from being a bully into a dork!" They both laughed.

Boris then quickly opened his notepad to show Gail his plan before she noticed him blushing.

Boris and Gail's
FORTUNE CLUB

… was written across the first page.

"We should start a business to help put your grandpa's stories into action! We could create something cool that has games, action sheets and even badges," said Boris.

"That's a great idea, Boris! Wow, you've changed so much. Remember when I first met you? You were kicking my flowers and hurting people. Now you are trying to help people!" replied Gail.

"I know. Before I met you, I never thought I could do anything good. Now after hearing about your grandpa, I feel I can do what he has done," said Boris with a smile.

"Would we be able to make money from helping others learn about money?" asked Gail.

"I'm sure parents would pay a small amount to make sure their kids started to look after their money as they grow up," said Boris. "My parents have already said they would happily have paid some money to learn what you have taught me, especially as it also helped them too."

"That's great. You know starting this business won't be easy; we are going to have to work really hard," said Gail.

"I don't care. I'm willing to work hard and, of course, we can work smart, like **Happy Hannah** and your grandpa!" Boris said. "I'm then going to follow the **Three Rules of**

Wealth so I can have my own Fortune Forest and become a gazillionaire."

Before they started working on their new business idea, they went to speak to Grandpa to make sure he was OK with them sharing his stories with other people.

"No way! I can't believe **I'M ACTUALLY GOING TO MEET YOUR GRANDPA!**" said Boris as he tried to control his excitement. Since hearing all the stories about his adventures on the island of Pucha-Pucha, Boris saw Gail's grandpa as one of his heroes. He was getting nervous about meeting him.

They walked up to Grandpa's house, where he was outside reading a book. As soon as Grandpa saw Gail, he got up to give her a big hug. "Have a seat. Let me go and get you some lemonade and cake. Granny will be home soon," said Grandpa.

Gail introduced Boris and told him she had been telling him all the stories about his adventures on Pucha-Pucha. They then went on to tell Grandpa about their business idea.

Grandpa was delighted to hear all the details. "This sounds like a great idea!" said Grandpa. "Starting your own business is a great way to earn some money and help people. Before you get started, is it OK if I tell you a story about how I tried to start a business on the island of Pucha-Pucha?"

"YES PLEASE!" said Boris excitedly.

Boris couldn't believe he was about to hear one of Grandpa's stories directly from Grandpa himself.

When I was on **Pucha-Pucha**, I was growing many different types of fruits which I sold at the market.

Whilst I was making money from selling my fruits, I was worried that if there was a big storm, I might be left with no fruits to sell. I really wanted to create something I could make all year round and sell, even if there was a storm. I just didn't know what to create.

Then I had some friends over for lunch. They had a little boy who was only one year old. I had nowhere for the little boy to sit. He ended up sitting on his mother's lap for the whole time.

That's when I decided I'd create highchairs for children on the island. As soon as my friends left, I worked on my new **HIGHCHAIRS**. I made loads of them as I had plenty of wood from all my trees. I was so excited as I thought so many people would buy them, and I'd have more money than ever.

Sadly, it didn't quite work out that way.

I put up a poster in the village and waited for everyone to turn up at my house asking for their very own highchairs for their kids, but **NO ONE CAME.**

I couldn't understand why they didn't come!

I thought it must have been my poster. I spent ages making it all colourful, with a good picture of the highchair. Still, no one came to buy any.

I then went into the village to see my friend Baker Bill at the bakery. He could see I was upset. I told him about the highchairs and my poster.

"I saw your poster. It looked nice, but look over in the corner. We already have three highchairs. We don't need any more," said Baker Bill.

"WHAT? How can you have highchairs?" I replied.

"DIY Doris has been making highchairs and selling them for ages. And they're a lot cheaper than yours," Bill told me.

I was so surprised. I hadn't seen any posters advertising DIY Doris' highchairs. It turned out she only put posters up in the village school—where all the parents who needed highchairs would see them. I hadn't seen the posters as I had been nowhere near the school. I didn't realise someone else was making the same thing, and they were selling it cheaper.

Initially I thought I could sell my highchairs cheaper than DIY Doris, or I could make sure my highchairs were better than hers. That was the only way I was going to get people to buy my HIGHCHAIRS. I then found out DIY Doris' highchairs were really good, and she wasn't earning much money from selling them. It would mean I wouldn't be making much money from selling them either, especially if I sold them at a lower price.

I was gutted as I now had all these highchairs that I'd made but couldn't sell.

I went back home and started picking my fruits again. It seemed like I'd only be able to make money from fruits, eggs, and milk.

As I was picking the fruits, I noticed a few were quite high up. I usually climbed the tree, but I grabbed one of the highchairs and stood on it. It was very **WOBBLY**, but then I added a few wood pieces to make sure it wouldn't break when I stood on it.

I could now reach more fruits without having to climb the tree. It made my life so much easier. As I was standing on my highchair, Nancy walked past and asked what I was standing on. I told her it was the highchair with a few extra pieces of wood to make it stronger. Nancy said, "I could really do with one of those. I hate having to climb my tree to pick the high-up fruits."

I grabbed another highchair, some wood and my hammer.

BASH! THWACK!
SLAM!

I'd added a few extra pieces of wood and gave it to Nancy.

The next day, I had a queue of people outside my house asking for one of my converted highchairs. Nancy had been telling everyone about hers. They were all willing to pay for the converted highchairs as it would make their lives so much easier.

That was how I started my **FRUiT LADDER** business. Instead of putting my poster up in the middle of the village. I put it up where I knew all the fruit pickers were.

Soon enough, I was making 'Fruit Ladders' in all different shapes and sizes.

GAIL AND BORIS START THEIR BUSINESS

"Thank you so much, Grandpa!" said Gail.

Gail and Boris left Grandpa's house to start working on their new business. "We need to make sure we learn from Grandpa's story," said Gail.

"You're right. We should make sure we check to see if people will buy what we are offering and then put up posters in the right places, " replied Boris.

In the weeks after meeting Grandpa, Boris and Gail did lots of **RESEARCH**.

They discovered there weren't many other websites with games and action sheets. Using these would help kids start taking action to grow their own **FORTUNE FORESTS** with their money.

They also discovered many parents were willing to pay to help make sure their kids learn about money, as it's not taught in most schools. They were going to start with their school friends in the village.

Boris and Gail worked on their business for weeks. When they didn't know how to do something, they asked their parents and friends. When their parents didn't know the answer, they simply said, "Let's find out together!" and sat down with them to research the answer on the internet.

"Let's make sure we have covered all the main points Grandpa has taught us," said Gail.

"Difference between being rich and being wealthy?" "**CHECK.**"

"Make sure all kids know they can become wealthy?" "**CHECK.**"

"Helping kids start their own business?" "**CHECK.**"

"The Three Rules of Wealth:

1. Keep one out of every ten seeds you receive.

2. Plant your seeds.

3. Let your trees grow." "**CHECK.**"

"Helping kids think about giving to charity?" "ooo**CHECK.**"

Boris and Gail were getting so excited. "It's all ready. Shall we press go?" asked Boris.

"*LET'S DO IT!*" said Gail.

"OK ...

WWW.FORTUNE-CLUB.CO.UK

... is now live!" said Boris. "I hope kids love it and we help them become great with money like your grandpa. Everyone should have their own Fortune Forest!"

Discuss with your Parents, Class, Friends and ...
I've honestly run out of other people!

Now you've finished the book, what actions are you going to take with your money?

GRANDPA'S MYSTERY CODE (14)

You should now have all of the letters to solve the code. Head over to Boris and Gail's new website, **www.fortune-club.co.uk**, enter the code and get access to two tools to help you become wealthy.

FINAL THOUGHT

WHENEVER

YOU HAVE MONEY, ASK YOURSELF:

What would

GRANDPA JACK DO ?

P.S. Did you know you've just

READ 21,339 WORDS

WELL DONE!

THE END

THANKS FOR READING

Glossary

ASSET ... is something you have which puts money into your pocket. Think of it as a tree which produces seeds. 'Investing' in a company is an asset. (Chapter 12)

CHARITY ... is when you give money (or time) to help other people who are in need. (Chapter 13)

DEBT ... is when you borrow money to buy something you can't afford yet. You have to pay back more than what you borrowed. Like when Richie Raccoon borrowed seeds from Mr. Credit Tree and had to give back a lot more as the red trees grew. (Chapter 8)

ENTREPRENEUR ... is someone who starts a business to earn money. Gail is an entrepreneur as she created and sold pictures made of petals to her friends. (Chapter 5)

GAMBLING ... is when you try to grow your money based on luck. Grandpa says that you never want to build your wealth using luck as you are most likely to end up poorer, not wealthier, over time. (Chapter 8)

INVESTING ... is when you use your money to own a piece of a company, or lots of companies, so your money can grow. (Chapters 7, 10 and 11)

LIABILITY ... something you buy that costs you money after you have bought it. Tiny Tina thought her Purple Tree (her home) was an asset but it was a liability as it cost her seeds to live in her Purple Tree. (Chapter 12)

PATIENCE ... is when you have to wait to get a reward. If you want to be wealthy, you have to be patient. (Chapters 8 and 11)

RICH ... is when you have money but spend most of it. Richie Raccoon was rich at the start of the book until he spent all his gold and couldn't find anymore. (Chapter 3)

SCAM ... is when someone tricks you to get your money, like when Shovel Sam tricked Grandpa Jack into believing there was gold on Pucha-Pucha just so he'd buy a shovel. (Chapter 2)

STOCK MARKET ... is the name of the virtual place where people invest their money. (Chapter 7)

TAX ... is when the government takes a bit of your money to help build schools, hospitals, roads and many other things which help the community. Grandpa Jack calls tax, Money Birds. (Chapter 9)

WEALTHY ... is when you have money and look after it so it grows over time. Grandpa was wealthy as his money grew whilst he slept. (Chapter 3)

A NOTE FROM THE AUTHOR

After qualifying as an Actuary, winning awards and spending close to twenty years advising large, global clients on investment strategies, I decided to write a story book for kids (and parents too!). How did I get to that?

A few years ago my wife and I decided to spend as much time as possible with our two daughters whilst they were young. "They only grow up once," as they say. So, when they were four and six, we decided to leave our full-time jobs for a few years to make this plan a reality. We were so grateful to have the financial freedom to be able to do this.

My wife and I were in this fortunate position because our parents had taught us from a young age how to look after money. This meant we saved and invested our own money over many years. As a result, the money we saved has grown, and it keeps growing even now, whilst we sleep.

I have come to understand just how critical it is to make the right choices with money from a young age, so, I want to share the stories about money I have been telling to my daughters since they were young. I want kids to grow up looking after their money and having the financial freedom that we are now enjoying as a family.

After reading this book, or having it read to them, I hope that ALL children grow up looking after their money and learning the simple actions they need to become wealthy and financially free.

This book is not just for kids. I hope that everyone who reads it—including parents, grandparents, and caregivers—learns something new about money. It's never too late to start looking after your money and making it grow.

Make sure you subscribe to our newsletter to continue to learn new ways to teach your kids about money.   For updates on future books and special offers visit: **www.bluetreesavings.com**

Will Rainey

Made in United States
Orlando, FL
04 April 2022

16458786R00150